FIVE YEARS AFTER 9/11

FIVE YEARS
AFTER 9/11

An Assessment of
America's War on Terror

Edited by
Julianne Smith and Thomas Sanderson

THE CSIS PRESS

Center for Strategic
and International Studies
Washington, D.C.

10102285

Cover photograph: Michael Rieger/FEMA News Photo

Library of Congress Cataloging-in-Publication Data
CIP information available on request
ISBN-13: 978-0-89206-492-2
ISBN-10: 0-89206-492-7

The CSIS Press
Center for Strategic and International Studies
1800 K Street, N.W., Washington, D.C. 20006
Tel: (202) 775-3119   Fax: (202) 775-3199
E-mail: books@csis.org   Web: www.csis.org/

CONTENTS

INTRODUCTION

Daniel Benjamin

In modern history, few if any events have had the instant, transformative impact of the terrorist attacks of September 11, 2001. In a matter of hours, the outlook of the United States changed profoundly. Gone were old beliefs about the almost unique security the nation enjoyed by virtue of its two ocean barriers to the east and the west and two friendly neighbors to the north and the south. Gone, too, were broad confidences in the safety of critical systems such as commercial aviation. Gone, as well, was the confidence that terrorism, an age-old and familiar phenomenon, would always be a tactic in which the attention of the many was focused upon violence against a very few.

America's response to the cataclysm was broad based, with massive initiatives undertaken in the belief that the global security landscape, as well as key national institutions, needed reshaping to provide citizens with better security. Accordingly, the United States quickly undertook military action against the Taliban regime in Afghanistan and, after that was deemed complete, against Saddam Hussein's Iraq. The first campaign was carried out because of the obvious connection between the Taliban and the al Qaeda authors of the 9/11 attack, who operated out of Afghanistan. Many different reasons were provided for the latter war, but the one the administration of George W. Bush has maintained throughout is that the fundamental conditions that breed terror could not be changed so long as Saddam's Baathist dictatorship remained in power. According to that argument, the frozen politics of the Middle East could only be shattered with a major military campaign in Southwest Asia. Together with the two wars, the U.S. intelligence and law enforcement communities, working with their partners around the world, set about destroying al Qaeda and allied groups through extensive clandestine and law enforcement operations.

At home, other efforts of enormous scope were begun, driven by the perception that the nearly two dozen agencies involved in providing for American homeland security were unable to perform the tasks if not consolidated and revamped. The resulting creation of the Department of Homeland Security was easily the most ambitious bureaucratic reorganization since the creation of the Department of Defense after World War II, and, given the breadth of activities for which the new department was to be responsible, this may have been an even more ambitious merger. Spurred by the findings of the blue-ribbon 9/11 Commission, a plan of reorganization was also enacted for the intelligence community.

Accompanying the renovation of U.S. government and military efforts were new elaborations of national strategy for dealing with the threat revealed by 9/11 and the reorientation and expansion of some activities to meet the requirements of the stated strategy. In the face of a powerful ideological challenge to the United States and the existing global order, the Bush administration sought to improve America's standing through a major upgrading of public diplomacy. Complementing the military and reconstruction effort in Iraq, the administration made democratization a central goal of its foreign policy, especially in the Muslim world.

These areas of endeavor hardly exhaust all the changes in American policy since 9/11, but they are representative of the core initiatives. The short essays that follow provide evaluations by CSIS scholars of the progress and the setbacks these efforts have encountered. They aspire to be both timely and balanced. Five years after the attacks, we have an ample basis for at least a first round of consideration of how the nation has fared with the challenges that were set on that fateful day. It is the authors' hope that the judgments presented here cast a light on this period that is both helpful and fair.

CHAPTER ONE

THE EVOLVING THREAT OF TERRORISM

Daniel Benjamin and Aidan Kirby

Any effort to draw up a balance sheet for the global war on terror must grapple with the problem of calculating gains and losses of many different kinds. Over the last five years, the United States and its partners have scored some notable headline-grabbing successes. At the same time, there is a strong argument to be made that many of those achievements have been fundamentally tactical in nature and that the overall picture is one of worrisome strategic slippage.

The single major exception in the plus column came very early in the conflict: the toppling of the Taliban leadership in Afghanistan, which robbed al Qaeda of the sanctuary it had enjoyed since the mid-1990s. During the time it was headquartered in Afghanistan, Osama bin Laden's organization managed through its financial largesse and loans of fighters to the Taliban to turn its host into the first terrorist-sponsored state. Al Qaeda was able to expand and strengthen its network and conspire against the United States and the West with relative impunity. Among the results, of course, were the destruction of two U.S. embassies in Eastern Africa, the bombing of the USS *Cole* in 2000, and the 9/11 attacks.

The invasion of Afghanistan in October 2001 culminated in al Qaeda's loss of its operational base. Consequently, the ability of bin Laden and his deputies to manage their network and direct attacks has been significantly degraded. The military campaign in Afghanistan was hardly perfect: the United States and its Afghan allies missed key opportunities to capture or kill terrorists, and the fact that bin Laden, his chief lieutenant Ayman al-Zawahiri, and others escaped represents a major failure.

The al Qaeda leadership, which is believed to be hiding out in the rugged Pakistan-Afghanistan border region, must now contend with a persistent threat to its security, which has undoubtedly had a cost for the terrorists. But bin Laden's ability to evade the United States has enhanced his standing in the broader Muslim world, seeming to confirm his claim to be spearheading a divine plan.

It is widely believed that the ability of the core al Qaeda group to carry out long-distance operations has been further reduced by the arrest or death of a number of high-level members. Early indications from the recently disrupted conspiracy to bomb American commercial aircraft flying out of London suggest that a formidable threat remains, though how directly al Qaeda individuals were involved has yet to be disclosed. Whatever the case, the group remains a threat, since the survival of only a small number of cells would allow it to carry out potentially spectacular attacks. Among the most notable cases of key al Qaeda operatives being put out of commission include the apprehension of 9/11 conspirators Ramzi bin al-Shibh and Khalid Sheikh Mohammed, perhaps the most innovative and dangerous terrorist planners in history, and the killing of Abu Musab al-Zarqawi in Iraq. Due to the remarkable coordination of intelligence services around the world, many cells of the original al Qaeda have been disrupted.

For all it counterterrorism accomplishments, however, the United States faces the unnerving fact that the ideology of jihad is spreading: A new generation of terrorists is emerging with few ties to al Qaeda but a worldview that derives from Osama bin Laden's vision of an unending war against the West. New areas of the globe are increasingly falling under the shadow of this growing threat.

So much is clear from the 2004 bombings in Madrid, the 2005 bombings in London, and the murder of Dutch artist Theo van Gogh by a young Dutch Muslim militant in the same year. These incidents demonstrate the rise of the new breed of self-starter terrorists, who are self-recruited and often self-trained, using the vast wealth of instructional materials available on the Internet. In contrast with the 1994–1995 Bojinka plot, in which a small group, probably numbering about six, planned to use liquid explosives in an attempt to blow a dozen U.S. airliners out of the sky over the Pacific, the 2006 Heathrow conspiracy appears to have involved 24 or more individuals. Unlike the Bojinka conspirators, they were not itinerant terrorists but primarily British citizens. Self-starters have appeared not only in Europe but also in Morocco, where they carried out a string of bombings in Casablanca in 2003, and in Pakistan, a country with a well-established jihadist infrastructure that some new recruits have deemed insufficiently aggressive. Attacks such as these undermine the Bush administration's claim that the United States would fight terrorists in Iraq and Afghanistan so it would not have to face them, as Vice President Dick Cheney put it, "in Washington or London or anywhere else in the world."

Geographically, the picture is one of jihadist metastasis. With more than 30 failed plots across the continent in roughly five years, Europe has become a central battlefield. In Australia, meanwhile, a major dragnet caught 18 conspirators who appear to have been plotting an attack on the country's one nuclear power plant. And in South Asia—as the recent bombings in Mumbai and a rash of violence in Bangladesh demonstrate—the incidence of Islamist violence has grown dramatically.

The U.S. failure to consolidate security in both Afghanistan and Iraq has since severely undermined the nation's early record of success. A resurgent Taliban represents an enduring threat to stability in Afghanistan, and perhaps the most damaging development is that Iraq has become the central battlefield of jihad. The number of foreign fighters in the country is disputed, but studies show that the insurgency against the U.S. occupation is drawing young men with no background in radical activities to Iraq. Even more ominously, an Iraqi jihadist movement has emerged where none existed before. Two of the major insurgent groups, the Islamic Army of Iraq and Ansar al-Sunna, embrace a radical ideology; al-Zarqawi's al Qaeda in the Land of the Two Rivers claims to have all-Iraqi units.

The chaos in Iraq has allowed for extensive training and development in various terrorist tactics and urban warfare, including increasingly proficient use of improvised explosive devices. Furthermore, the proliferation of such tactics—thanks to traveling fighters and information sharing via the Internet—has ensured that the style of urban warfare tactics will likely be exported to distant regions. Where the collapsed state of Afghanistan allowed numerous opportunities for bin Laden's endeavors, the ongoing insurgency in Iraq has produced a new type of threat: a real-time, authentic "jihad" experience that is grooming a new generation of committed fighters.

The implications in the Middle East/Persian Gulf region of so much jihadist activity in Iraq are ominous. In November 2005, three hotels in Amman were bombed by Iraqi suicide operatives, the first major attacks in Jordan and the most stunning demonstration yet of the spillover effect of the turmoil in Iraq. But they were hardly the only such cases. Kuwait, a country with no history of jihadist violence, experienced running gun battles between authorities and militants and discovered plotters within its own military. Syria, a country that waged a campaign of extermination against Islamists in the early 1980s, has seen Sunni radicalism reemerge. Qatar experienced its first vehicle bombing in early 2005. Saudi Arabia suffered a series of bombings and attacks, and though the authorities have gained the upper hand against al Qaeda on the Arabian Peninsula, the group still exists. The discovery of Iraqi-style bombs in the kingdom may well be a harbinger of worse to come once veterans of the fighting to the north return home, especially because Saudi Arabia has contributed the largest number of foreign fighters to the Iraqi insurgency.

There is a significant possibility of wider destabilization because Iraq's terrorists appear to have won a sanctuary in the overwhelmingly Sunni-dominated al Anbar province. U.S. troops have fought one campaign after another in this region, from the villages on the Syrian border to cities such as Ramadi and Fallujah. Yet terrorist attacks have often increased because the militants shrewdly move out of town when troops arrive and return after our forces depart. They will be rooted out only when there is a capable Iraqi intelligence service. Since that service is likely to be dominated by Shiites and Kurds, there are not going to be many operatives able to work in the hostile environment of al Anbar. The likelihood is that this sanctuary will be there for years.

It is not obvious now how many Iraqi jihadists will support the global jihad of bin Laden and how many will focus their efforts on Iraq's fledgling state. Even if relatively small numbers opt for the global fight, though, it could make a significant difference to the terrorists' capabilities, as has been seen by the actions of the small numbers of individuals involved in the Madrid and London bombings.

The chief reason for the spread of the jihadist ideology is the failure to deal effectively with the ideological component of Islamist radicalism. Although administration leaders have often spoken of the terrorists' ideology of hatred, our actions have too often lent inadvertent confirmation to the terrorists' narrative. In its most barebones formulation, that narrative holds that the United States and its allies seek to occupy Muslims' lands, steal their oil wealth, and destroy their faith. Radical Islamists interpret much of history through this prism: from the redrawing of borders in the Middle East after World War I to the creation of Israel to the U.S. deployment to Saudi Arabia and the invasion of Iraq in Operation Desert Storm. Radical Islamists believe, moreover, that the United States supports the autocrats of the Muslim world as a way of keeping the believers down and undermining the faith.

More than anything else, U.S. actions in Iraq have given the radicals fresh fodder for their "clash of civilizations" claims. Polling in Muslim nations over the last three years has shown that America's image has plummeted to historic lows. In Jordan, a key U.S. ally, for example, the percentage of poll respondents who say they have a positive opinion of the United States has reached as low as 1 percent in recent years. In Pakistan, a U.S. ally of long standing, which possesses nuclear weapons, favorable sentiments have improved in the past two years: the figures for 2006 show that 27 percent of Pakistanis have a favorable opinion of the United States, but the same figure in Jordan is only 15 percent. Although the overwhelming majority of Muslims will not turn to violence, in this environment it appears more are turning in that direction as actors or supporters than would otherwise be the case. It is clear that Iraq provided a major part of the motivation for the Madrid and London bombers and for Mohammed Bouyeri, the murderer of Theo van Gogh. In countries such as Pakistan, it is also clear that anti-Americanism has been bolstered by the invasion of Iraq, and it is increasingly being used as a tool of mobilization for radicals.

Moreover, the effectively unilateral invasion and the botched occupation opened a new "field of jihad" for militants who were more than eager to take on U.S. forces in the Arab heartland. For the radicals, killing Americans is the essential task; by doing so, they demonstrate that they are the only ones determined to stand up for Muslim dignities. Through their violence, they have also created a drama of the faith that disaffected Muslims around the world can watch on television and the Internet. Thus, the jihadist movement's show of its determination to confront American and coalition forces, as well as those of the fledgling Iraqi regime, has boosted its attractiveness. However benign our intentions were in going into Iraq, in the context of the culture of grievance that exists in much of the Muslim world, the extremists' narrative has had a profound resonance. In this environment, moderates who might normally be pro-Western have been silenced by the widespread disdain for the occupation in Iraq. The key goal of any counterinsurgency—to separate moderates from extremists—has thus been unattainable.

The United States has been fortunate not to have been struck again since 9/11, and a number of reasons can be adduced for this. The American Muslim community has thus far been largely immune to the jihadist virus. It is more difficult for radicals from abroad to gain entry to the country. Al Qaeda is on the one hand not as capable and on the other hand determined that its next attack will top its last one in drama and impact. And, of course, it is easier for jihadists to kill Americans in Iraq than it is in the United States, and those casualties provide the radicals with the proof they need to show the global community of Muslims of their devotion to their cause. Over the long term, however, the terrorists will inevitably seek to rebuild their networks and capabilities to attack the United States at home. This is the gold standard for them, and if the overall strength of the movement is growing, reestablishing the capacity to carry off "spectaculars" will be on their agenda.

CHAPTER TWO

IDEOLOGY AND THE BATTLE OF IDEAS

Julianne Smith and Karin von Hippel

When the United States called for partners in a global campaign against terror in the days following the 9/11 attacks, the response was overwhelmingly positive. Dozens of countries, from longstanding allies to traditional competitors, swiftly offered a wide range of economic, political, legal, and in some cases, military support. Months later, as the United States began to outline a concrete agenda for its war on terror and the president turned his focus toward Iraq, the outpouring of sympathy from every corner of the globe subsided, and questions and suspicions about U.S. intentions intensified. By early 2003, hundreds of demonstrations against the United States and its plans to go into Iraq were being held in cities around the world. In just a year and a half, the United States went from being perceived as a global leader to a global menace. Despite predictions about a new era of international cooperation, global public opinion had reversed course, and Washington found itself increasingly isolated and criticized even by longstanding allies.

Since the invasion of Iraq, global public opinion about the United States has remained well below the pre-9/11 average. Beyond the invasion itself, a series of events, ranging from the human rights abuses at Abu Ghraib prison to allegations of torture at the Guantanamo Bay detainment camp, combined with the poorly planned and implemented reconstruction of both Afghanistan and Iraq, have severely damaged the United States' credibility and image. Foreign public opinion polls show that pluralities in a number of countries feel that the U.S. presence in Iraq is a danger to world peace. For example, according to a poll conducted by the Pew Global Attitudes Project in June 2006, 41 percent of Britons believe that the U.S. military presence in Iraq is a great danger to stability in the Middle East and world peace, while 34 percent feel the same way about the current government in Iran. In Spain, the numbers are 56 percent and 38 percent respectively. A 2005 University of Jordan poll found that "Arabs uniformly and strongly oppose U.S. policies towards Iraq." They believe that the U.S. government wants to control Iraqi resources, and that U.S. policy will not result in democracy in the country nor in improvements in the lives of ordinary Iraqis. As a result, the U.S.-led war on terror, once widely supported by countries on every continent, has been greatly discredited and is increasingly viewed as anti-Islam.

Determined to counter profound anti-Americanism worldwide, the U.S. government commissioned dozens of studies in the years following 9/11 to determine why the world—particularly the Middle East—feels so negatively toward the United States and what can be done to reverse that trend. Time and again, the overarching message that emerged from such reports was the need for a greater emphasis on public diplomacy and better use of "soft power" tools to win "hearts and minds." Accordingly, the U.S. government embarked on a robust public diplomacy strategy that aims to reflect U.S. values. It increased resources for public diplomacy and launched a rapid response capability and joint initiatives with the private and nonprofit sectors. The U.S. administration also publicly committed to democracy promotion efforts to bring stability and peace to many corners of the world that foster hate and promote violence. How have these efforts fared since 9/11?

PUBLIC DIPLOMACY

Over the last few years, new public diplomacy initiatives have been instigated, although thus far with limited success. As a first step, the State Department created an under secretary for public diplomacy and public affairs, elevating public diplomacy on the U.S. foreign policy agenda. However, that office has suffered from a number of false starts over the past five years, wasting precious time and resources as attitudes have hardened. Charlotte Beers, the first to hold the post, tried to counter negative images of the United States with the Shared

Values Initiative, which included an advertising campaign depicting religious tolerance and moderate Muslims in the United States (which several Arab nations refused to run). Beers left in 2003 and was replaced by Margaret Tutwiler, who left just five months into the job.

Nearly four years after September 11, in the summer of 2005, Karen Hughes, a longtime and close adviser to President Bush, was asked to return to Washington to breathe fresh life into the ailing public diplomacy program. Hughes quickly embarked on a strategy of "engage, exchange, educate, empower and evaluate," created partnerships with businesses and foundations, introduced "echo chambers" to provide ambassadors with messaging guidance, and reached out to women and youth. She also set up the Interagency Strategic Communications Group and established a regional public diplomacy hub in Dubai.

In addition to creating the post of under secretary for public diplomacy, the U.S. government started a handful of media outlets in the Middle East: the Arabic-language Radio Sawa (which has been sending pop music and news into the Middle East since March 2002), the Persian-language Radio Farda (which beams political and cultural news into Iran) and Al Hurra, a satellite TV channel created in 2004 to counter Al Jazeera. Modeled after Voice of America (VOA) and Radio Free Europe (RFE), these stations are designed to promote pro-American attitudes and democracy.

None of these newly created stations appears to be having much of an impact. Unlike RFE and VOA, which were staffed by well-known émigré intellectuals, Radio Sawa's Lebanese broadcasters have been criticized for their poor grammar, and Sawa's reporting has been called "uneven" by the State Department's inspector general, though it appears to have the most popular appeal, in part because it broadcasts pop music. (It is estimated that over 20 million people listen to Radio Sawa each week.) In late 2005, U.S. broadcasting efforts lost considerable credibility when it was revealed that the Pentagon was secretly funding a radio station and a newspaper in Iraq and paying Iraqi reporters to write pro-American stories.

The U.S. government and the nongovernmental sector have also started a series of dialogues, exchange programs, and listening tours to foster mutual understanding. The challenge with these programs comes in identifying the appropriate partners. Does one choose those that are already sympathetic to U.S. views (often elites) or those who are openly critical of U.S. policies? Currently, at least at the government level, there seems to be a preference to engage so-called moderates, such as journalists, professors, or judges. Of course, there is always the risk that these same people might be advocating a more extremist view behind closed doors. The key is to find partners that have popular appeal, who might influence political developments and public opinion.

Another challenge with dialogue and exchange has been access. U.S. embassies, in an effort to protect their staff, now resemble unwelcoming fortresses. Physical barriers, combined with tighter controls on student visas and the false assumption that foreigners, particularly Muslims, are not welcome in the United States, led to a sizeable drop in the number of foreign students in the first few years after 9/11. (Between 2001 and 2003, the number of student visas fell by almost 30 percent.) Thanks to the efforts of then Secretary of State Colin Powell and a group of senators, among others, this trend is slowly being reversed, although the accessibility of U.S. embassies remains an issue.

In early 2006, Secretary of State Condoleezza Rice launched the Transformational Diplomacy Initiative, which will reposition at least 100 foreign service officers from Europe to difficult assignments in the Middle East and Asia. The program will also require foreign service officers to accept two of these difficult assignments before being promoted to the senior ranks. Foreign service officers will have a choice between assignments in traditional embassies or in a number of newly created one-person posts in cities such as Alexandria, Egypt. While it is still too early to assess the success of this particular initiative, a number of analysts state that it is long overdue and will likely lead to a much stronger presence in the countries where public opinion is the most adverse to the United States.

Despite the efforts of Hughes and others over the last year, majorities in the Muslim world continue to view America in a negative light (although recent polls have shown a slight improvement in America's image in several countries). Because world opinion is so closely tied to actual U.S. policies, one has to be realistic about the degree to which any public diplomacy program can change attitudes. That said, a well-designed, properly funded and targeted program could help mitigate the problem. Most efforts to date, however, have not yet reversed the negative image of the United States; indeed some have reinforced it.

Several changes should be made in the years ahead. First, Hughes's office needs an overarching strategy with measurable objectives and clear guidance on worldwide implementation. The strategy should provide country-specific guidelines that distinguish between various social, economic, and political environments and identify key influencers. Second, although funding for public diplomacy programs has increased 57 percent since 2001, Hughes's office still lacks sufficient resources. Her headquarters staff numbers only a few, and the $1.2 billion dollars dedicated to public diplomacy in 2005 is not enough to cover much-needed exchange programs, send speakers around the world, and ensure that public diplomacy officers receive the language training they require (the GAO reports that 30 percent of language-designated public diplomacy posts are filled with officers who lack the required language skills). Hughes will receive an increase of $68 million in 2007, but relative to other U.S. funding, whether it be the military budget, Iraq, or even U.S. assistance to Afghanistan and Pakistan, it is evident that public diplomacy remains a low priority among appropriators.

In addition, the U.S. government needs to be more strategic with the resources it does have for public diplomacy. That requires designing a strategy with quality controls and evaluations. Initiatives to date (such as *Hi! Magazine* and Charlotte Beers's infamous advertising campaign) failed in part because the people working on public diplomacy have little to no training or experience in the Muslim world and a dearth of practical experience to draw on. Overall, the public diplomacy campaign seems to be heading in the right direction, after a shaky start. U.S. democracy promotion efforts may also require more strategic focus in order to ensure that the reality catches up with the rhetoric.

BUILDING DEMOCRACY

The U.S. government has been involved in state-building and promoting democracy for over a century. From the end of the Cold War, the promotion of democracy has been a priority for all U.S. administrations, with the ultimate aim being the enhancement of international peace and security.

Since 9/11, democracy promotion has also been advocated as one way to attack the "root causes" of terror and to prevent weak states from being penetrated by international terrorist cells. The U.S. National Strategy for Combating Terrorism (February 2003) declared, "we will ensure that efforts designed to identify and diminish conditions contributing to state weakness and failure are a central U.S. foreign policy goal. The principal objective...will be the rebuilding of a state that can look after its own people." It concluded, "diminishing these conditions requires the United States, with its friends and allies, to win the 'war of ideas,' to support democratic values, and to promote economic freedom." The 2006 National Security Strategy explains: "The goal of our statecraft is to help create a world of democratic, well-governed states that can meet the needs of their citizens and conduct themselves responsibly in the international system."

The U.S. government has set out to do this through several main reforms—including bureaucratic changes such as upgrading the administrator of the U.S. Agency for International Development (USAID) to deputy secretary and director of foreign assistance and establishing within the State Department the Office of the Coordinator for Reconstruction and Stabilization—in an attempt to join up all parts of government involved in post-conflict operations. Democratic reforms should be streamlined through this more joined-up approach, with regional initiatives, such as the Middle East Partnership Initiative (MEPI), focusing on tailored reforms.

While it is too early to review the management changes, more can be said about the policy of democracy promotion over the past five years. Here, the results thus far have been less encouraging, due to three reasons: poor anticipation and analysis, a lack of integrated strategies, and unclear measures of progress.

Poor anticipation and analysis of the consequences of democracy promotion has in fact already led to some adverse results, particularly in parts of the Middle East and North Africa, where anti-American Islamist parties have gained seats through the ballot box. Examples include the election of Hamas in Palestine, Hezbollah gaining a number of seats in the 2005 elections in Lebanon, increased representation for the Muslim Brotherhood in Egypt, and Islamist parties performing well in Morocco, Algeria, Iraq, and Kuwait. The overall success of the Islamist parties can be attributed to a number of factors, but U.S. pressure for democratization in the Middle East, the war in Iraq, and anti-regime sentiment (with the U.S. government viewed as closely tied to these regimes) have also factored into these successes. In most cases, the Islamist parties were more successful at mobilization techniques and had built up grassroots support over the years through Islamic charities, which provided much-needed services to the population. The habit, particularly with Arab regimes, of allowing religious parties to operate while secular parties are often shut down or constrained in their activities, also accounts for the success of the Islamist organizations.

Analysts of the region have been predicting this result for some time. Had their warnings been heeded, democratization efforts might have focused on political party building for moderate parties, anti-corruption measures, or media training, for example, before elections were held. At the same time, it is also possible that the Islamist parties will become less radical while in power due to the need for compromise, assuming they respect the democratic process.

Outside the Middle East, U.S. rhetoric is not matched by integrated reforms, and democracy promotion has been given a low priority, particularly in cases of weak and collapsed states. In Somalia, for example, which is the most egregious example of state collapse, and a place where the United States worries about terrorist penetration, the U.S. National Strategy has not been followed. The total amount spent in Somalia by states of the Organization for Economic Co-operation and Development (OECD) over the past five years has hovered at approximately $100 million to $150 million per year, with the bulk of funds dedicated to humanitarian programs. The U.S. contribution to development in Somalia—which includes governance funds—has been only $2 million to $5 million dollars per year during this same period.

In Pakistan, a country of key strategic concern, funding for democratization programs is not aligned with the priority given to this effort within the broader U.S. foreign policy agenda. While democracy promotion funds have increased considerably, with the U.S. government appropriating $30 million for Pakistan in 2007, this comprises a small part of the overall declared U.S. assistance package of $1.4 billion. The bulk of funding is security related, with many security goals impeding democratization strategies. Undoubtedly, the high priority placed on keeping this nuclear-armed country stable and resilient in the face of growing religious radicalism explains a great deal in terms of the allotment of resources, though it might be asked whether such a policy is not also somewhat counterproductive. In other parts of Central Asia, short-term security goals take precedence over longer-term gains that would result from embedding democracy in the region.

Finally, and similar to the public diplomacy campaign, the U.S. government still has not developed reliable measures of progress as part of its overall strategy. Indeed, the goals of democracy promotion are often vague, outreach poor, information on the ground unreliable and rumor filled, and the measures of progress too dependent on individual efforts or the direct result of these efforts—such as a new hospital, rather than on the overall impact of the strategies, such as improved health care. The politicization of metrics—where reports of success or failure are not grounded in a generally accepted methodology and instead become little more than political spin—continues to interfere with accurate accounting of progress.

Together, these deficiencies have contributed to inconsistent and unsatisfactory outcomes. Indeed, the democracy promotion campaign has not achieved the goals set by the U.S. government since 9/11. In fact, even the aid has failed to win over public views: The 2005 University of Jordan poll found 73 percent of national samples in five Arab states agreed that the "U.S. aims to dominate countries by offering aid"; 61.6 percent agreed that the "U.S. always violates human rights in the world"; and only 26.8 percent agreed that the "U.S. supports the practice of democracy." If instead the U.S. government can improve its anticipation and analysis, implement integrated strategies, and develop reliable measures of progress, democracy promotion will achieve greater success.

CHAPTER THREE

AMERICA'S DOMESTIC SECURITY

David Heyman and Eric Ridge

The images of American Airlines Flight 11 and United Airlines Flight 175 crashing into the World Trade Center's twin towers will be forever etched into the American psyche as a turning point for the United States. There is perhaps nothing more emblematic of or more central to the 9/11 attacks than the airplanes. Suicide bombers converting hijacked airplanes into guided missiles shattered the U.S. illusion of invincibility at home and of nation-states as the principal threat to America's security. But beyond the iconic implications, the use of airplanes as weapons, the indiscriminate targeting of civilians, and the quest to inflict maximum casualties demanded the most dramatic rethinking of U.S. security at home and abroad in nearly half a century.

To the government's credit, in an instant, the prevention of the next terrorist attack was catapulted to the forefront of the U.S. policy agenda. September 11 was seen not as an isolated incident, but as one in a series of attacks in a long, previously unrecognized war against America, reaching back to the bombings of the U.S. Marine barracks in Lebanon in 1983, the first World Trade Center attack in 1993, and the 1998 destruction of the U.S. embassies in Kenya and Tanzania. And the president and his team seized on this understanding. Fighting a twenty-first century enemy that is unconstrained by the conventional limitations of a nation-state, the Bush administration believed, would require a controversial strategy: to engage in a fight of terrorist enemies abroad so that Americans would not have to face them at home. In the resulting Global War on Terrorism, U.S. efforts have killed or captured most of the al Qaeda leadership responsible for the 9/11 attacks, seized hundreds of millions of dollars of terrorist assets, and reportedly disrupted a number of terrorist plots against the United States.

But despite these tangible achievements, terrorism has neither been quelled nor conquered. To the contrary, terrorist recruitment and terrorist attacks continue to expand unabated. Homegrown terrorism is on the rise in Europe and North America, and the attacks in Madrid and London, along with the more recent disruption of attacks in Australia, Canada, and again in London, belie the notion that fighting terrorism abroad will prevent it at home. Rather than relenting, the spread of radical Islamist ideology has hastened, gaining traction in fragile democratic states from Lebanon to Indonesia and driven in no small measure by the perceived sense of grievance generated by the U.S. presence in Iraq. Countering threats abroad cannot substitute for strengthening protection at home.

The United States has made notable strides on the domestic security agenda since 9/11, establishing new institutions such as the Homeland Security Council (HSC), the Department of Homeland Security (DHS), the Transportation Security Administration (TSA), and the National Counterterrorism Center (NCTC). America has devoted significant new resources to counter biological threats, nuclear smuggling, and attacks on commercial aviation; improved border screening; and stimulated new efforts to expand state and local capacity to prepare for and respond to attacks.

New institutions and new resources are a necessary part of strengthening domestic security, but they are not sufficient to build a new domestic security infrastructure. For all its accomplishments, the federal government's efforts to protect America at home have failed to articulate an overarching homeland security architecture, one with a specific structure, requirements, priorities, and timelines for implementation. Today, the most important question—are we prepared?—cannot be answered, mainly because the government's response to the terrorist threat remains by and large ad hoc and incomplete. Specific efforts to reorganize the government; to communicate threats to the public; to engage Americans on what it means to be prepared; and to prioritize among diverse and disparate security threats are, after five years, still deficient and reflect a government responding to the "crisis du jour" rather than executing a comprehensive and unified homeland security strategy.

DHS AND NEW GOVERNANCE

If airplanes were the symbols of a changing international threat environment, the TSA—Transportation Security Administration—and new TSA airplane passenger screenings represented the transformation of U.S. domestic security. The need to protect commercial air travel from another attack was first among post-9/11 reforms. To accomplish this, Congress passed the Aviation and Transportation Security Act in November 2001, creating the Transportation Security Administration. With TSA, the government federalized security-screening operations at all commercial airports and air terminals, hiring and training 56,000 employees to take over passenger and baggage screening from private companies, eliminating the fact or perception that the nation's aviation security was the responsibility of the lowest bidder for the government contract. And even if future hijackers could somehow bypass security, new air marshal programs, hardened cockpit doors, and armed pilots would be put in place to defeat them.

Although screening under TSA has had a mixed record, a number of notable gaps in aviation security have persisted since its founding. First, TSA still has not adopted technology to screen for liquid explosives—a shortcoming made even more urgent by the recent foiled attempts in London. In 1994, Ramzi Yousef, who masterminded the 1993 World Trade Center bombing, and Khalid Sheikh Mohammed, who planned the 9/11 attacks, conceived of a plot to sneak liquid explosives onto a dozen planes headed to Seoul and Hong Kong and then to the United States. The Bojinka plot, as it was known, was foiled, but history shows that al Qaeda returns to early targets or compromised plans.

Other gaps in our nation's aviation security persist as well. Under the Aviation and Transportation Security Act, TSA would provide for screening of all property, including all cargo, carry-on, and checked bags. Yet less than 15 percent of cargo in the belly of commercial planes is screened to determine if explosive materials have been brought on board. And beyond commercial aviation, there is general aviation (GA)—that is, all aviation other than military and commercial airlines. Though GA is a significant part of our national aviation system, there has been no government-led systematic review of general aviation assets—airports, aircraft, and operations—from a security standpoint, nor recommendations for any priorities of additional protection. The private sector has taken a number of steps to enhance the security of general aviation, but in comparison to the extensive investments in protecting commercial aviation, general aviation has not received the attention it needs by the federal government.

Creating TSA was a highly visible, but in the end, relatively small piece of a much larger government-wide reorganization. One of the most significant questions to emerge from the ashes of 9/11, beyond how to protect commercial aviation, was how the U.S. government should organize to protect against and combat catastrophic terrorism writ large. Did the United States' vulnerability to terrorism stem from a failure of intelligence, or did it suggest a more fundamental, system-wide weakness? Was the patchwork of local and federal law enforcement authorities, with a minor military component, sufficient to protect the nation?

The administration's initial approach to domestic security was to create two new White House institutions. Under Executive Order 13228 (issued October 8, 2001), the president established a new Homeland Security Council (HSC) that, notwithstanding the parallels on paper with the National Security Council (NSC), would have neither the power nor the influence of the NSC. The president also created the Office of Homeland Security, whose staff was charged with the nearly impossible task of corralling the multitude of homeland security–related federal agencies, armed with limited funds and no legal authority.

Despite pressure from Congress and recommendations from several Commissions,[1] the administration took 14 months to reorganize federal resources and create the Department of Homeland Security (DHS). Setting up the department marked a crucial first step toward consolidating homeland security missions under one roof and providing a management infrastructure for policy development and resource allocation. But three years after this merger—admittedly, one of the largest in history, encompassing 22 separate agencies and 180,000 employees—the department is still bogged down with day-to-day start-up issues such as finding a permanent headquarters to house the full complement of—and now distributed—DHS leadership, integrating management information systems, and developing a unified, accountable acquisition system. The department also continues to face tremendous hurdles trying to align and de-conflict turf-conscious bureaucrats, protecting their legacy missions and budgets.

As a result, DHS has been unable to focus adequately on some of the important changes that the reorganization made possible. For example, unlike the vast majority of the new department, which was composed of legacy agencies imported from elsewhere in government, the Directorate of Science and Technology (S&T) was one of the truly new innovations. A 2002 National Academies' report, *Making the Nation Safer: The Role of Science and Technology in Countering Terrorism*, provided a blueprint for countering asymmetric terrorist threats with asymmetric advantage: harnessing America's unmatched scientific ingenuity and technological prowess to benefit homeland security operations. But, three years after the department's creation, the S&T directorate remains in many respects an island, insufficiently connected to the customers inside and outside the department who set the requirements for, and deploy the products of, the department's research and development. A means to move promising technology from the research side of DHS to its field operations is urgently needed.

Similarly, managing the sharing and analysis of intelligence among the federal government's homeland security stakeholders was one of the most touted requirements after 9/11. However, this mission has proceeded with fits and starts, having been the reason for no fewer than three major restructuring efforts over the last five years. The Homeland Security Act contemplated a central role in information sharing and analysis for DHS in the Intelligence Analysis and Infrastructure Protection (IAIP) office. But that office was not up to the task, and the administration instead created a new stand-alone Terrorist Threat

Integration Center (TTIC), which later became the National Counterterrorism Center (NCTC). The NCTC has provided a far better bridge than the Department of Homeland Security to narrow the gap between the CIA, FBI, and other intelligence community players, thus addressing one of the primary contributing factors to the United States' failure to piece together the 9/11 plot and alert appropriate agencies to counter it.

WARNING, WARNING, WARNING: CHARACTERIZING THREATS AND ALERTING THE PUBLIC

Although the CIA and FBI may now be better at sharing information with each other, sharing threat information outside the federal government—to essential stakeholders such as cities, states, private industry, and the public—has bogged down over leadership shortfalls, a lack of policy articulation, turf wars, and technological incompatibility. Moreover, progress has been stymied by the government's continued inability to reconcile national security needs with civil liberties requirements.

In March 2002, in order to help translate actionable intelligence into public warnings to federal, state, and local authorities and to the American people, the federal government created the color-coded Homeland Security Advisory System (HSAS). And in 2004, DHS launched its Homeland Security Operations Center (HSOC) to evaluate and disseminate the most urgent information about any kind of threat and to help coordinate the immediate response to any emergency. By design, the government would use a set of graduated color-coded "threat conditions" to provide warnings to the public or eventually to specific cities or sectors as the risk of a threat increased. In turn, federal agencies, state and local governments, the private sector, and citizens would then implement corresponding "protective measures" to bolster defenses. Although the framework made sense, the system was overused and poorly explained during its first two years of operation. This led to threat fatigue among some local officials, who simply stopped following federal guidance, and among the wider public, which was provided no actionable information and thus left helpless to decipher what the changing threat levels meant and how to react.[2]

The failure to engage the public effectively to prepare for and respond to terrorism underscores a major deficiency today: the lack of capacity to communicate with citizens in the event of an imminent or ongoing crisis. Emblematic of this was a May 2005 incident, when a small, private plane flew into restricted airspace within miles of the U.S. Capitol. No public warning was issued, nor was a system available or even capable of doing so. While officials at the HSOC communicated the threat to federal agencies, they failed to involve or even notify District of Columbia officials stationed in the HSOC with them. Nor was the mayor of Washington informed. As a result, the public did not know about the event or whether to shelter in place or to evacuate. Ultimately, congressional staff were evacuated into the streets and open spaces surrounding the Capitol, putting them in harm's way had the oncoming plane been shot down over their heads. Had this incursion been a chemical or biological attack instead of the false alarm it turned out to be, the government would have possessed no reliable method of communicating instructions to the public.

PREPARED FOR WHAT? TO BUILD A HOMELAND SECURITY SYSTEM OR NOT

With all the institutions that could be transformed, all the investments and training that could improve our nation's preparedness, and all the critical infrastructure that could be secured against future attacks, the task of building and implementing a new domestic security architecture is daunting. Policymakers are faced with tough questions: in the absence of known threats against specific targets, where should we begin? What are the most important steps to take? What are the most important assets to protect?

Given plausible threats and possible targets, America's vulnerability is nearly endless: attacks could come by air, land, or sea using conventional explosives or nuclear, chemical, biological, or radiological weapons to target any geographic region or sector. Targets could include agriculture, the defense industrial base, energy infrastructure, public health and healthcare delivery systems, national monuments and icons, banking and financial institutions, drinking water and water treatment systems, commercial facilities, dams, emergency services, transportation systems, government facilities, or nuclear reactors, materials, and waste. Terrorists could also execute cyber attacks against many of these same targets.

America's national focus must be to differentiate between "tolerable" hazards and catastrophic threats—those that pose the greatest risk of inflicting mass casualties, massive property loss, and immense social disruption. For domestic security, the goal must be to prioritize investments and put in place protective measures to prevent and defend against those scenarios that pose the greatest risk. It is a balancing act: risk can never be eliminated, while resources are always limited. So policymakers must make prudent choices.

During the past several years, Congress has supported models that favor directing funds to home districts over risk-based resource allocation, while the Department of Homeland Security's attempts at a risk-based formula—which is the right idea—indefensibly cut funding for Washington, D.C., and New York, two high-risk cities, by 40 percent. Consequentially, many areas where the threat, vulnerability, or possible consequences are high and well-established—chemical facilities and ports, for example—remain inadequately protected.

One of the greatest recent risks, and one in which early public warning could not have been clearer or timelier, was Hurricane Katrina. The storm, whose path, magnitude, and potential for destruction were forecast with extraordinary accuracy, not only starkly illustrated the United States' lack of preparedness for a predictable catastrophe, but called into question how the nation would have performed in the event of a surprise terrorist attack.

By the time of Katrina, the federal government had taken a number of steps to implement a National Preparedness System, as called for by the Homeland Security Act of 2002. Homeland Security Presidential Directive-1 (HSPD-1) created the Homeland Security Council, and HSPD-3 the Homeland Security Advisory System. Additional presidential directives developed standards and strategies for critical infrastructure protection (HSPD-7), biodefense (HSPD-10), maritime security (HSPD-13), and domestic nuclear detection (HSPD-14).

Among the most significant of these steps was the March 2003 presidential directive to establish a single, comprehensive all-hazards approach to manage domestic incidents. The resulting National Incident Management System (NIMS), and associated National Response Plan, completed in December 2004 and put into effect in the summer of 2005, codified federal roles and responsibilities and established a uniform command structure for on-scene crisis management during an incident. It also provided the architecture by which the federal response to Katrina was later to be managed (or not managed, as the case may be)—an architecture that turned out to be overly complicated to implement and had to be revised again in May 2006.

Separately, HSPD-8 (December 2003) attempted to clarify what preparedness meant by calling for development of a National Preparedness Goal. This goal was to "establish measurable readiness priorities and targets that appropriately balance the potential threat and magnitude of terrorist attacks, major disasters, and other emergencies with the resources required to prevent, respond to, and recover from them." The final draft of that goal, which envisions a more comprehensive homeland security system, was released in the first quarter of 2006 but lacks timelines and deadlines and has yet to be implemented.

Each of these presidential directives, taken individually, provides a piece of the response needed for catastrophic terrorism. But collectively they do not constitute the National Preparedness System that Congress mandated, any more than an assemblage of bones and organs would constitute a human being. The development of the United States' homeland security system has been more ad hoc than strategic, and the basic questions that everyone should be able to answer today—preparedness for what, accomplished by when, and completed by whom and how—have yet to be answered.

CONCLUSION

In the five years since 9/11, U.S. policymakers across all levels of government have devoted massive resources—time, energy, and money—to protecting U.S. citizens from terrorist attacks. At the federal level, the task of organizing for domestic security led to the largest federal restructuring since 1947, in the form of a new cabinet-level department charged with coordinating and leading national domestic security programs. State and local governments have also done their part, dramatically increasing spending on security and expanding capacity to prevent and respond to terrorist attacks. As a result, from symbolic national landmarks like the Empire State Building and the Washington Monument, to high-visibility venues such as stadiums and parades, as well as to border crossings and certain critical infrastructure, defenses are better today than five years ago.

Does that mean we are better protected? Certainly. But are we safe? Maybe not. The terrorist threat continues to grow, and the broader strategy that integrates offensive counterterrorism overseas with protective measures at home remains unwritten. As the spread of radical Islamist ideology continues, we have not countered with the architecture or resources to establish a truly national homeland security system and preparedness program that integrates federal, state, and local governments, in addition to private firms and citizens. Nor do we know what it means to be prepared. Numerous challenges lie ahead. Indeed, it has become increasingly clear that America must redouble its efforts to reduce domestic vulnerabilities, strengthen protective measures, and build a society that will be resilient in the face of future attacks. We must also confront the true causes of radicalization if we are to reduce its spread, not just combat it. During the past five years, the United States has made important strides. But we must move much faster and accomplish much more during the next year and years to come, or we may yet again find ourselves the victim of catastrophic terrorism.

Notes

[1] The three leading commissions looking at post–Cold War national security strategy and with a particular focus on terrorism included the U.S. Commission on National Security in the 21st Century (the so-called Hart-Rudman Commission), the Gilmore Commission, and the National Commission on Terrorism. The February 2001 Hart-Rudman Report, *Road Map for National Security: Imperative for Change*, recommended establishing a National Homeland Security Administration based on their concern that: "The combination of unconventional weapons proliferation with the persistence of international terrorism will

end the relative invulnerability of the U.S. homeland to catastrophic attack. A direct attack against American citizens on American soil is likely over the next quarter century. The risk is not only death and destruction but also a demoralization that could undermine U.S. global leadership. In the face of this threat, our nation has no coherent or integrated governmental structures."

[2] In one such case, Homeland Security Secretary Tom Ridge said the danger of a terrorist attack was low on the same day that Attorney General John Ashcroft appeared on national television to say that al Qaeda was "almost ready to attack."

CHAPTER FOUR

─────────

INTELLIGENCE

James Lewis and Mary DeRosa

The 9/11 attacks propelled intelligence reform to center stage in American politics. September 11 was an immense failure for U.S. intelligence, prompting Congress and the executive branch to respond with initiatives that promise reinvention and, perhaps, revitalization.

The centerpiece of reform is the reorganization mandated by the Intelligence Reform and Terrorist Prevention Act of 2004 (IRTPA). IRTPA was the culmination of a series of proposals to reform U.S. intelligence that began with the Boren/McCurdy initiative of 1992. The common elements of these proposals were the need to strengthen the director of central intelligence and to adjust U.S. intelligence efforts to meet new kinds of threats. Between 1990 and 2001, there were many proposals for reform, but little progress.

September 11 provided the impetus to move ahead. The 9/11 Commission's epic 2004 report seared the CIA for its failures and put intelligence sharing and a coordinating authority at the center of its recommendations for change. Congress wrote these two recommendations into IRTPA. The new law was also shaped to a surprising degree by ideas from business management. Its reforms are not sui generis, but part of a larger trend to modernize the federal government by adopting business practices. The concepts of information sharing and an enterprise architecture (restructuring a corporation to unify the efforts of its business units) for the intelligence community undergird the reform effort. The intelligence community in the United States is composed of many competing organizations; IRTPA's overarching goal is to meld these organizations into an integrated intelligence enterprise with a common mission and a powerful CEO.

Critics point out that, in the final regard, faced with opposition from the White House and the Department of Defense, Congress introduced ambiguous language and potentially crippling compromises into the legislation. Though the new director of national intelligence (DNI) is more powerful than the director of central intelligence, the DNI continues to share authority over intelligence activities with the secretary of defense, the attorney general, and the director of the FBI. Nor has the DNI's staff (in many ways an expanded version of the old and often ineffective Community Management Staff) yet gelled into a powerful coordinating body.

The new superstructure for intelligence faces many challenges. Chief among them is ensuring that information needed to prevent another catastrophic attack is collected and shared. In this, there has been some progress. Even before Congress passed IRTPA, the FBI and CIA (the most important of the counterterrorism agencies) began doing a much better job of working together in the war against terror. The new National Counterterrorism Center created by IRTPA has improved coordination and analysis on terrorist intelligence. Though the larger effort at information sharing among intelligence agencies has lost momentum, there has been progress in this important area. Aggressive global action by the reenergized and refocused FBI and CIA is the primary reason there has, so far, been no repetition of 9/11 in the United States, despite unremitting efforts by determined enemies—a success that is largely independent of IRTPA's reforms.

Much remains to be improved. First, the intelligence community's analytical capabilities are still uneven. The report of the commission on U.S. intelligence capabilities and Iraq's weapons of mass destruction (WMD) highlighted systemic problems in analysis. The community operates in a herdlike fashion. A previous set of intelligence reforms, reacting to the groupthink that distorted intelligence in the Vietnam War, tried to build in options for dissent, but an analyst who resists the herd's conclusions still does so at his or her own peril. Another problem involves deceit. Saddam tricked the United States and others. His regime might have lasted longer if he had cooperated with the UN, but he chose to bluster and lie. Analysts, swayed by Iraq's long involvement with WMD, did not question his deceptions. There is no simple cure for this kind of mistake, and our opponents are increasing their efforts to deceive and dissimulate. Finally, the experience with Iraq and WMD showed that when the United States does not like a country, it taints analysis. No scenario is too improbable if biases and dislike can lead analysts to abjure the necessary skepticism that must always be applied to intelligence.

It is comforting to imagine that the misreading of Iraq and WMD was the result of partisan distortion. Washington appreciates this kind of morality play, as it is easy to plot a happy ending. Keeping politicians and their staff out of analysis is always a good idea, but it is not enough. Problems like herd behavior, deceit, and dislike contaminate analysis. These problems are difficult to fix, particularly if we pretend they are not there. IRTPA's organizational reforms do not address analytical weaknesses. The interim solution to the problem of weak analytical capabilities in the intelligence community has been to rely, to a startling degree, on analytical services provided by private contractors.

There are also serious problems with the collection of intelligence. As with analysis, these problems predate 9/11, but the attack gave a greater sense of urgency to improving both technical and human collection. The organizational reforms of IRTPA do not address many of these collection problems, perhaps on the assumption that the more powerful DNI and more integrated intelligence community created by the act will make the needed repairs.

Public discussion of intelligence reform has paid less attention to technical collection, but this is where the United States spends the bulk of its money and gets the bulk of its classified information. Reforming technical collection is an immediate priority for the DNI. The United States has spent hundreds of billions of dollars since the 1950s to build massive technical collection systems—chiefly for "sigint" (signals intelligence) and for imagery collected from space. The United States designed this collection architecture for large, static, conventional military opponents, and it worked reasonably well against them. These collection systems are less effective against nimble opponents

who blend easily into civilian populations, but that is only one problem. Technological change has eroded collection capabilities. The
United States' opponents are now much more aware of technical collection and routinely seek to evade it, often with success. None of these
problems are irremediable (particularly for sigint), but progress will
require approaches that blend intelligence disciplines and adopt new
technologies for collection.

Conventional wisdom suggests that the solution to the declining
value of technical collection is to increase our capability for "humint"
(human intelligence or intelligence collected by the classic techniques
of espionage). Humint reached its nadir in the 1990s. Stations were
closed, the clandestine service shrank, and the number of U.S. spies
reached a historic low. Direct support to military operations was em-
phasized at the expense of other missions. Worse yet, a culture of ti-
midity and legalism seeped into clandestine work. Well-intentioned
guidelines on agent recruitment, for example, were interpreted to
mean that the CIA could no longer enlist individuals with question-
able backgrounds. Unfortunately, it is often these individuals who are
willing to become agents and have access to needed information.
George Tenet, director of central intelligence from 1997 to 2004, did
much to reverse these damaging trends, but rebuilding the clandestine service remains a national priority.

Some in Congress argue that the United States should change intelligence budget priorities to spend less on technical collection and
more on espionage. Instead of satellites, they argue, the nation needs
more of its citizens to become spies, wearing keffiyahs and sneaking
into Osama's tent to hear the big plan. The premise—strengthening
humint—has merit, but the prescription Congress draws from it is
wrong.

Throwing money only goes so far in rebuilding espionage capabilities. Spying needs professionals. To be professional, spies need experience, and that experience cannot be bought. It must be gained
through apprenticeship and practice. There is also a limit to how
many spies a country can usefully deploy. The number of U.S. agents
fell far too low in the 1990s, but above a certain number, spies compete
with each other for the best sources. They trip over their counterparts

from other agencies, or put third-rate informants on the payroll to show they are doing their job. There are only so many potential foreign agents available for recruitment, and adding more case officers or more money will not change this. Some of these problems may lessen if the new National Clandestine Service, created to manage all humint activities overseas, proves to be effective.

The environment for clandestine work is also more challenging. The United States has greatly strengthened international cooperation with foreign intelligence agencies to meet the jihadist threat, building on relationships that predate 9/11. However, the international context for U.S. intelligence activities has become decidedly unfavorable in the last five years. The European Parliament investigates and condemns CIA operations. Italy has gone so far as to arrest its own chief of military intelligence for cooperating with the United States and issued warrants for 21 Americans it believes were involved in the capture of a terrorist living in Milan. The unremitting hostility U.S. intelligence agencies face from broad sections of the European political spectrum affects both operational capabilities and the larger U.S. diplomatic effort, and the reputation of U.S. intelligence in many parts of the world where we must operate and find cooperation is worse than it has ever been.

The problems with analysis, collection, and coordination are significant and will preoccupy the DNI and the White House for years to come, but the chief dilemma for reform lies in the conduct of domestic intelligence. The increased importance of domestic intelligence in the fight against terrorism raises many thorny questions. Effective counterterrorism must avoid the cumbersome handoffs between foreign intelligence and domestic law enforcement that crippled our initial responses to al Qaeda. Terrorism transcends national boundaries. Terrorists operate in the United States. For this reason, the line between foreign and domestic intelligence that we have long recognized in our laws and policies no longer makes sense. But the line's purpose was to protect civil liberties; if it is gone, what protections will take its place? None of the significant reform efforts to date addresses those questions. IRTPA simply sidestepped the issue. Passage of the Homeland Security Act provided no answers either; no one believes that the new Department of Homeland Security, given its many weaknesses, should be in any way responsible for leading domestic intelligence.

Domestic intelligence is an uncomfortable problem. Americans do not like domestic spying, and a long series of unhappy experiences—the Red Scare of 1919, McCarthyism, COINTELPRO, and Watergate—shows that there is good reason for this dislike. The legal structure that shapes U.S. domestic intelligence activities grew out of Watergate-era concerns over a White House that used intelligence and law enforcement assets for domestic political ends. Now, however, this legal structure is fracturing under the pressure of Islamic terrorism.

The president's decision to use the National Security Agency (NSA) to conduct surveillance on domestic telephone calls, without the blessing of the Foreign Intelligence Surveillance Act (FISA) Court created by 1970s reforms, highlights fundamental problems that failing to address the issue have caused. The administration found that the authorities for domestic communications surveillance and oversight were inadequate to its needs. Its solution was to assert that the president's constitutional authority allowed him to engage in domestic surveillance without approval of the FISA Court. Congress, in its oversight role, was either acquiescent or supine. The result has been controversy and uncertainty.

In the debate leading to IRTPA, there was some discussion of creating a U.S. equivalent of MI5 (the UK service for domestic intelligence), but the idea did not advance very far. Establishing a new agency charged with domestic surveillance would have created serious risks to civil liberties, and aligning its authorities with constitutional protections would have been an arduous task.

Expanding the FBI's role in domestic intelligence avoids the many dilemmas concerning oversight, court authorization, and the relationship between intelligence gathering and police powers that a new domestic intelligence agency would face. It also avoids the upheaval that creating yet another major new agency would cause. The administration took a step toward strengthening the FBI's domestic intelligence effort in 2005 when, using existing authorities and resources, it directed the FBI to merge its intelligence, counterterrorism, and counterintelligence divisions into a new National Security Branch (NSB). However, some doubt the FBI's ability or enthusiasm for this task, and it is unclear whether restructuring the FBI alone is sufficient for effective counterterrorism.

That the president thought it necessary to take these actions with the NSA and FBI suggests that IRTPA's reforms are irrelevant to or inadequate for the most pressing task the intelligence community faces—preventing another 9/11. Finding a way to confront terrorists, who may be citizens and who operate with equal ease inside and outside the United States, without damaging civil liberties will require a long and thorny examination of whether and how to change the daunting thicket of laws that surround intelligence. IRTPA's unspoken hope was that reorganization and information sharing would provide enough improvement to obviate the need for a difficult debate on how to conduct intelligence in a world where foreign and domestic are no longer meaningful distinctions. If the war on terror drags on for a generation, as some predict, this debate will be unavoidable.

Discomfort and tension between an open and legalistic democracy and the practice of intelligence is inevitable. This discomfort helped to drive intelligence reform in the 1970s, and it still resonates in the public debate. However, the threat today is immediate and direct, as 9/11 made clear. Further reform is still essential. An intelligence apparatus designed to operate against other government bureaucracies is ill-suited for the inchoate and globally diffuse opponents we face today. Globalization increases our opponents' capabilities and shortens the time available to detect, warn, and prevent. Reorganization is not reform, although it can provide the means and opportunity for change. Our metric for success must be improved performance by the intelligence services, including the FBI. IRTPA and the work of the DNI and his staff are only the start of a complex process for improvement. While we may find this process difficult to complete, success in intelligence reform will make the difference between surviving the war on terrorism and winning it.

CHAPTER FIVE

_____

INTERNATIONAL COOPERATION

Thomas Sanderson and Mary Beth Nikitin

Since 9/11, terrorist attacks have occurred on virtually every continent, highlighting the global nature of the threat and the global cooperation required to counter it. Terrorist activity stretches across a bewildering variety of cultures, locations, languages, criminal linkages, support networks, and financing mechanisms. The expertise and tools needed to counter or prevent such activity therefore rests with no single nation but can be found among a variety of nations, institutions, and individuals. While a plethora of coalitions, large and small, have been formed over the last five years (with varying degrees of success), the most pressing case for international cooperation concerns the proliferation of weapons of mass destruction (WMD). International experts sometimes dispute the likelihood of terrorists acquiring WMD, but few doubt they would be used if acquired; therefore, preventing the proliferation of WMD to terrorists is one of the most urgent priorities for the global community.

GLOBAL THREAT, GLOBAL RESPONSE

When the World Trade Center towers fell in New York City, the world felt the impact and reached out to Americans with genuine sympathy and solidarity. Soon after 9/11, 800 million people in 43 European countries observed several minutes of silence. Millions of Muslims also held vigils. Prior to the invasion of Afghanistan, Iran quietly agreed to provide sanctuary for American forces in distress on their border. Syria and Libya shared intelligence with their U.S. counterparts, and even Fidel Castro and Kim Jong Il expressed their outrage and offered limited assistance. Tremendous goodwill and sympathy were bestowed on America in the face of an unprovoked attack.

At the United Nations, member states—more than 80 of which lost at least one citizen to the attacks on September 11—responded quickly with Resolution 1373, passed on September 28, 2001, and mandating a specified number of counterterrorist measures. With more than 140 nations taking action in some respect, the response to the terror attacks was timely and extensive, if uneven. Consider also the original military coalition built after 9/11, which contributed to the overthrow of the Taliban in Afghanistan. While multinational ground forces prepared for action in Kunduz and Kabul, NATO invoked Article V of its charter, and soon alliance personnel were patrolling U.S. skies in AWACS radar planes. Most European countries, including France and Germany, clamored to lend a hand.

But in the lead-up to the March 2003 invasion in Iraq—an invasion the United States was linking directly to the Global War on Terrorism (GWOT)—the attitudes of many of those same UN and NATO members turned uncooperative and even hostile. Millions of people in more than 60 countries marched for peace and against U.S. intentions. The "coalition" that defeated Saddam's Iraq was in reality an alliance composed of the United States and the United Kingdom, with limited help from several other states. In Iraq, unlike in Afghanistan, the Pentagon was desperate to expand this list of partners, especially in the post-combat, reconstruction phase. The turnaround in public sentiment and multinational support was profound. The invasion of Iraq was advertised as a necessary and core element of the GWOT, but it is considered by many to have worsened the positive trends in international cooperation immediately following 9/11.

A steady stream of U.S. rhetoric alienated allies and others. Absolutist terminology such as "good" and "evil" and "you are either with us or against us" were seen to be devoid of nuance and middle ground in a confrontation that most other nations did not see as black and white. U.S. policies sharply emphasizing the role of the military or appearing to disregard international law and sovereignty were seen as blunt and counterproductive in the competition for the moral high ground.

In addition, some international cooperation has led to dubious arrangements as well as association with serious human rights abuses. America's embrace of Uzbek president Islam Karimov linked the United States with that leader's ruthless internal security practices. The United States was eager to gain access to the Khanabad air base in Uzbekistan for operations against Taliban forces in Afghanistan. This arrangement, and others like it, may have served the United States' tactical, near-term needs, but they also undermined its long-term strategic goals. With such examples, the world perceived a disconnect between America's core values and foreign policy.

Some U.S. actions have even pitted various foreign government departments against one another. One European nation's role in the suspected CIA rendition of terrorist suspect Abu Omar now has that country pursuing criminal charges against its own military intelligence service, in addition to issuing arrest warrants for 21 U.S. intelligence officers believed involved in the operation. Likewise, the alleged U.S.-funded secret prisons for terrorism suspects in Eastern Europe have prevented greater foreign participation and public support of the U.S. global counterterrorism campaign. The United States' own abuses at Abu Ghraib prison and detentions at Guantanamo Bay have significantly eroded America's credibility as the guarantor of due process and human rights. These actions have imperiled the United States' success and relationships. As a result, European publics are pressuring their governments and the European Union to limit or stop cooperation with the United States.

To be certain, there are a number of bright spots in the record of international counterterrorism cooperation. Though marked by many ups and downs, the United States has worked closely with the United Nations to harmonize members' counterterrorism practices. The United States has coordinated successfully with financial institutions and organizations such as the Financial Action Task Force to detect and freeze terrorist funds and transactions. The six-country Alliance Base counterterrorism unit in Paris, strongly supported by French president Jacques Chirac despite his reservations about Iraq, is also an example of good intelligence sharing and joint operations. Intelligence officials and analysts from the United States and other countries report that steady and effective cooperation has been the rule over the last five years. Middle Eastern and Central Asian partners have provided some of the best intelligence resources where the United States sometimes has few. Jordanian intelligence played a key role in the successful pursuit of Abu Musab al-Zarqawi, while Pakistan was pivotal in the apprehension of several high-ranking al Qaeda leaders within its borders.

Military, legal, and law enforcement assistance programs are also meeting with noteworthy success. In Southeast Asia, the United States (in partnership with Australia) has worked closely with Indonesia, the Philippines, Malaysia, and Thailand. Information exchanges and technical assistance are credited with diminishing the terror threat in Indonesia specifically and in the region more generally. Law enforcement cooperation has been constructive, but less so than among intelligence agencies. Problems with sharing evidence and information for prosecutions, and the highly public disapproval of U.S. rendition practices, have complicated some of these programs and relationships.

Additional international cooperation highlights include the U.S.-funded Trans-Sahara Counterterrorism Initiative. This project provides Niger, Mali, Chad, and Mauritania with training to detect and challenge terrorists attempting to transit the vast Sahel region of Africa. Also, the ongoing threat to commercial aviation from man-portable, surface-to-air missiles is being addressed with U.S. leadership and pressure. Since 2003, 18,500 missiles in 17 countries have been destroyed. Unfortunately, several thousand have gone missing from Iraq's pre-war stockpile.

GLOBAL EFFORTS TO PREVENT CATASTROPHIC TERRORISM

Initially, it appeared that global cooperation to prevent the proliferation of WMD would be another success story in the campaign against terrorism, with the birth of global initiatives and high-level political statements pledging new dedication to preventing catastrophic terrorism. However, evidence was mounting that the threat itself was evolving.

At least two al Qaeda operatives were arrested attempting to acquire what they thought was highly enriched uranium (HEU), a key material needed to make a crude nuclear device. Technical documents discovered at al Qaeda safe houses in Afghanistan in November 2001 included basic information on nuclear weapons design, the physics of nuclear explosions, and the properties of the nuclear materials needed to make such weapons. Rudimentary laboratories and manuals for chemical and biological weapons were also uncovered. Osama bin Laden has asserted a "religious duty" for al Qaeda to seek nuclear weapons, and prominent radical clerics have in recent years declared their belief that the use of weapons of mass destruction is permissible against "infidels." In 2004, revelations about the A.Q. Khan network raised the specter of an extensive nuclear black market that might help terrorist ambitions become realities. All of this provided more than enough cause for the international community to take urgent action.

But as the campaign turned to Iraq and the search for WMD there, North Korea and Iran fell out of the headlines, and international focus on the nuclear ambitions of these two players faltered. Meanwhile, North Korea and Iran have both advanced their nuclear capabilities with potentially destabilizing impacts on regional and global security dynamics. Iran's connections to terrorist groups are well documented. North Korea's erratic behavior, illegal activities, and missile sales to states that are clear supporters of terrorism, are well known. Concerns persist that proliferation from these states to non-state actors could occur, with or without the regimes' knowledge. Analysts also fear scenarios where unstable regimes are toppled and the WMD materials or weapons they possess are left unsecured and vulnerable to diversion.

The United States has been working with allies to defeat the nuclear ambitions of Iran and North Korea. France, the United Kingdom, and Germany (the "EU-3") have pursued a negotiated settlement with Iran since the August 2002 public revelation of a clandestine nuclear program in that country. Yet, after more than three years of inspections and investigation, the International Atomic Energy Agency (IAEA) remains unable to verify that Iran's nuclear program is for purely peaceful purposes, and tangible results have yet to come from the negotiation process. After years of open skepticism, in the spring of 2006, the United States moved to support the EU-3 by offering direct talks with Iran about its nuclear program. On June 6, the EU-3, China, Russia, and the United States jointly asked Iran to suspend its uranium enrichment program as a sign of good faith and as the precondition for negotiation on the future of the Iranian nuclear program, to include a package of incentives offered by the six countries. The UN Security Council passed Resolution 1696 on July 31, requiring Iran to halt all enrichment and reprocessing activities and comply with the IAEA's demands by August 31, threatening further council action if Iran did not comply. High-level Iranian officials have so far indicated that Iran would not give up its uranium enrichment capability, and the Iranian government has not yet responded to the U.S. offer of direct talks.

While the July unity of the Security Council is encouraging, much of the world remains skeptical of the United States' belief that Iran is pursuing nuclear weapons, in no small part due to the recent memory of faulty intelligence on Iraq's WMD programs. The United States has been slow to support multilateral engagement to prevent an Iranian nuclear weapons program, and the current solidarity is tentative at best. Furthermore, while the proposal on the table offers Iran incentives and an economically viable plan for receiving nuclear fuel from Russia for a civilian program, it is not clear whether Iran will accept these terms, or whether penalties such as economic sanctions encourage compliance or resistance. The United States and its allies all seek a nonnuclear-armed Iran, but Washington has not yet laid out a comprehensive strategy to achieve that goal.

The United States is pursuing negotiations with North Korea on a multilateral basis. The "Six Party Talks," involving the United States, Russia, Japan, China, the Republic of Korea (ROK or South Korea), and the Democratic Peoples Republic of Korea (DPRK or North Korea), were opened in August 2003, after North Korea admitted to a clandestine uranium enrichment program in violation of the 1995 Agreed Framework, withdrew from the Nuclear Non-Proliferation Treaty (NPT) and began to reprocess the plutonium that had been in internationally monitored storage since 1994. The Six Party negotiations still struggle to find traction after a number of setbacks, including Pyongyang's February 2005 declaration that it had "produced nuclear weapons." A diplomatic breakthrough was thought to have been achieved in September 2005 when the Six Parties agreed on a statement of principles that committed North Korea to abandoning all nuclear weapons, returning to the NPT, and allowing safeguard inspections by the IAEA "at an early date." But shortly thereafter, these results were discounted by Pyongyang due to disagreement over the sequencing of North Korean dismantlement and in reaction to the strengthening of international financial sanctions that target the North Korean leadership's personal assets. In July 2006, North Korea launched seven short- and medium-range missiles, including their Taepodong 2, in defiance of calls for restraint by the international community. The launch led to UN Security Council Resolution 1695, requiring all UN member states to end transfer to North Korea of any goods or technology that could contribute to its missile or WMD programs. Many analysts fear that North Korea's need for hard currency, history of illegal activities such as drug trafficking, and illicit technology transfers might cause it to sell its nuclear material or technology to terrorists or other "rogue" states.

In light of these state proliferation challenges and their potential links to non-state actors, as well as the heightened perception of the risk of WMD terrorism since 9/11, the United States has jump-started a number of international coordinating mechanisms to bolster WMD counterproliferation and proliferation prevention programs.

Improving capacity for WMD interdiction and export controls has been given increasing attention, although it remains difficult to measure results. In May 2003, the United States introduced a program of coordinated land, sea, and air interdiction—the Proliferation Security Initiative (PSI)—in response to the growing threat posed by the spread of WMD, their delivery systems, and related materials. Initially, Australia, France, Germany, Italy, Japan, the Netherlands, Poland, Portugal, Spain, and the United Kingdom agreed to the PSI Statement of Interdiction Principles. Today, more than 70 countries have endorsed the initiative and promised their voluntary participation. The PSI retains no explicit legal authority, emphasizing instead the need for states to strengthen existing laws and regulations regarding interdiction. The PSI Operational Experts Group, which includes military, law enforcement, intelligence, and legal experts, meets to plan joint interdiction-training exercises, share expertise, and expand cooperation to key industries. While interdiction cooperation between the United States and other countries occurred before PSI existed, the exercises and regular dialogue are meant to make such interactions routine and strengthen capacities in other countries.

The seizure of the German-owned vessel, the BBC China, in October 2003, in which authorities found 1,000 centrifuges of Pakistani origin destined for Libya, illustrated the importance and potential impact interdictions can have on interrupting illegal WMD trade. After years of quiet talks between the United States, United Kingdom, and Libya, the BBC China capture catalyzed Mu'ammar Qadhafi's decision to acknowledge and allow the verified destruction of Libya's WMD programs in December 2003.

One of the more troubling discoveries revealed during the dismantlement of Libya's nuclear program was the origin of its nuclear equipment and knowledge. With Libya's cooperation, officials were able to disrupt the illicit nuclear supply network headed by the father of the Pakistani nuclear bomb, A.Q. Khan. The "Khan Network," set up to supply Pakistan with technologies for its own weapons program, was selling centrifuges, bomb designs, and other nuclear weapons–relevant technology in what had become a "Wal-Mart of private-sector proliferation," in the words of IAEA director general Mohamed ElBaradei. After Khan was put under house arrest in Pakistan, he immediately confessed on Pakistani TV to running an international proliferation ring and aiding the nuclear programs of Libya, North Korea, and Iran. He was pardoned the next day by President Pervez Musharraf. Pakistani authorities have prevented outside access to Khan and continue to deny any complicity in his actions. Due to Khan's isolation, the full scope of his dealings remains a mystery. There may still be remnants of his network operating and attempting to supply illicit nuclear technology on the black market. The United States has chosen not to press Pakistan on this issue, so as not to jeopardize Pakistan's cooperation in counterterrorism operations along the Afghan border or destabilize the already fragile government. However, until the full scope of

Khan's network is known, there will be no certainty that it has been fully shut down. On a parallel track, the United States has been quietly providing assistance to secure Pakistan's nuclear facilities.

In response to the A.Q. Khan revelations, the UN Security Council passed Resolution 1540 in April 2004 requiring all countries to tighten their internal controls on WMD materials and implement strict export controls. There has been limited progress in implementing this resolution beyond a partial submission of documentation to the UN. Developing countries will require financial and technical assistance to fulfill the requirements of the resolution and sustained diplomatic engagement to ensure that the laws are indeed implemented.

Denying terrorists access to WMD materials and weapons as the most effective way to prevent catastrophic terrorism has gained traction in rhetoric if not always in action. At the first summit of the Group of Eight nations (G-8) following 9/11, the world leaders announced the Global Partnership against the Spread of Weapons and Materials of Mass Destruction. The G-8 countries pledged $20 billion over 10 years ($10 billion from the United States) to secure or remove materials where they are housed, beginning with an acceleration of work in Russia. While this effort has increased the participation of non-U.S. donors to cooperative threat reduction, the pledges still fall short of the $20 billion promised, and little of this money (only about 18 percent) has been turned into actual projects. Moreover, most of the projects under way are not focused on addressing the most serious risks of nuclear and biological terrorism prevention.

On a global scale, the world has only just begun to organize work effectively to prevent nuclear terrorism. Weapons-grade nuclear materials are now present in 135 civilian research reactors in 40 countries globally. Presidents George W. Bush and Vladimir Putin announced the "Global Initiative to Combat Nuclear Terrorism" at their bilateral summit in St. Petersburg, Russia, this summer. This initiative is meant to rally international partners to coordinate efforts to secure, remove, and dispose of vulnerable nuclear materials worldwide, as well as to better coordinate existing border security and detection programs.

The United States, Russia, and the IAEA continue to work together to "clean out" weapons-grade uranium from civilian research reactors worldwide under the Global Threat Reduction Initiative, which the United States formally launched in May 2004. The program's broader goals are to identify, secure, recover, and facilitate disposition of vulnerable high-risk nuclear and radiological materials around the world. Progress has been made, particularly in the past year, in returning highly enriched uranium from U.S.- and Soviet-supplied research reactors, including 186 kilograms of Soviet-supplied HEU removed from facilities in eight countries. While intense efforts are under way to repatriate all Soviet-supplied HEU by 2010, the pace of these efforts is not commensurate with the urgency of the threat. All U.S.-supplied HEU is not to be repatriated until 2019, and 45 percent of research reactors currently using HEU are not slated for conversion or shutdown. The United States will need to cooperate with other donor countries to create package incentives and provide technical assistance to countries hosting these reactors. Moreover, there is still no accounting for what quantities of nuclear materials exist elsewhere in the world. Without such a baseline, it is difficult to set priorities for clean-out efforts, measure progress on securing these materials, or evaluate the severity of the threat they pose.

The United States should be applauded for its efforts over the past five years to raise the profile of WMD proliferation prevention, devote more resources to it, and create innovative international cooperation tools to address the threat. However, actions by the United States have not always supported its strong rhetoric, and many endeavors lack a firm international legal basis. Also, the United States has neglected traditional multilateral nonproliferation tools and fundamentally ignored the underlying causes of proliferation. U.S. declarations and initiatives are only as good as the follow-up actions taken. The director of national intelligence testified to Congress in early 2006 that al Qaeda remains interested in acquiring chemical, biological, radiological, and nuclear materials or weapons to attack the United States, U.S. troops, and U.S. interests worldwide. Governments have not moved fast enough to secure and reduce WMD materials around the world considering the determination of terrorist groups to acquire WMD and the catastrophic consequences if they were to succeed.

CHAPTER SIX

U.S. STRATEGY AND CAPABILITIES FOR WINNING THE LONG WAR

Michèle Flournoy and Shawn Brimley

Five years after the horrors of 9/11, the United States is still struggling to create an effective strategy commensurate with the challenge posed by radical Islam and the capabilities required for success in this long war. There is a significant gap between the strategy the administration appears to be following and the capabilities it has created and utilized in pursuit of it. Unless this gap is bridged, victory will remain elusive.

Grand designs and noble goals are necessary, but wholly insufficient in the absence of a comprehensive roadmap for linking aspirations to actual programs and connecting capabilities to resources. Without the connective tissue between strategy and capabilities, the United States is left with what one analyst has termed "a two-country solution to a 60-country problem." The absence of an effective strategy has led to an overutilization of military and covert action tools and a notable underutilization of other instruments of national power that are vital to success against a dangerous ideology.

Irrespective of where one stands on the efficacy of the foreign policy choices of the current administration, the possibility of strategic failure increases as the gap between strategy and capability widens.

Our nation badly needs better capacity for strategic planning, as well as more resources for the vital nonmilitary capabilities that must be created in order to enable victory. Policymakers need to do a better job of integrating ends, ways, and means. Above all, better orchestration of our instruments of national power is a prerequisite for success in this long war.

The essential first step in winning the long war is developing a clear and compelling strategy—one that reflects the fundamental nature of the struggle in which the United States is now engaged. In the Cold War's early years, the government, academia, and think tanks made an extraordinary effort to understand and characterize the Soviet threat. In fact, some of the most important early thinking of this period was led by President Dwight Eisenhower himself—with the so-called Solarium Project—and engaged members of the cabinet and the National Security Council staff in developing U.S. grand strategy for the Cold War.

Since 9/11, President Bush has issued and revised the U.S. National Security Strategy and signed a number of National Security Presidential Directives (NSPDs), but he has not articulated a grand strategy for this new long struggle. NSPD-46, signed in March 2006, characterizes the threat from Islamic extremists and identifies a number of U.S. policy objectives for dealing with it. The administration's National Implementation Plan further details U.S. objectives for the long war, as well as associated tasks to achieve these objectives. The plan also assigns lead and supporting agencies for each task and instructs them to develop their own supporting plans. Indeed, some agencies, like DoD, have given new weight to the long war in their strategy and planning documents. The department's 2006 Quadrennial Defense Review (QDR) placed substantial emphasis on the need for the U.S. military to hone its capabilities for "irregular warfare" and to help build the capacity of partner governments to deal with threats of terrorism and insurgency.

In principle, NSPD-46 and the National Implementation Plan were supposed to yield an integrated government strategy for the United States. In practice, however, they have fallen far short of this goal. The National Security Council has devoted too little attention to prioritizing the myriad objectives articulated in these and other administration documents related to the long war. Consequently, agencies lack clear guidance on where to place emphasis and where to accept or manage a degree of risk when, in the absence of unlimited resources, not everything can be given equal importance.

In addition, the question of how various means of national power should be used to complete specified tasks and achieve specified ends has not been adequately addressed. Still lacking are interagency concepts of operation that delineate how various agencies will work together to achieve the unity of effort necessary to be effective in the long war.

Furthermore, the mechanisms that Congress and the administration have established to integrate the efforts of disparate and fiercely independent agencies remain weak. Although the National Counterterrorism Center (NCTC) is charged with integrating "strategic-operational" planning and overseeing execution, its newness, relative weakness, and location outside the normal chain of command hamper its ability to perform these functions. Nor has any feedback loop been created to ensure that any gaps or shortfalls in U.S. capabilities identified by the NCTC are addressed in future budget cycles.

In practice, these gaps and shortfalls have contributed to a profoundly imbalanced U.S. approach to the long war. The administration has consistently overemphasized the role of the military, without adequately using or resourcing other instruments like intelligence, law enforcement, diplomacy, information operations, trade, and foreign assistance, which are equally critical to victory. Moreover, it has focused its energies on Afghanistan and Iraq rather than prosecuting a truly global campaign against radical Islam. Finally, it has taken a largely retail approach to fighting terrorist organizations like al Qaeda—focusing on capturing or killing known terrorists and cells—rather than a more wholesale approach directed at preventing the recruitment of subsequent generations of terrorists by addressing root causes.

In contrast to its insufficient efforts to devise an effective strategy, the administration, together with Congress, has created numerous new capabilities since 9/11 to protect the country and prosecute the long war. From the intelligence reforms that produced the director of national intelligence and the National Counterterrorism Center, to the creation of the Department of Homeland Security, the breadth of change is impressive, but it remains unclear whether the United States has all the capabilities it needs for success.

September 11 added momentum to several ideas that had existed prior to the attacks—creating a Department of Homeland Security and establishing a director of national intelligence. The 2002 Homeland

Security Act and the 2004 Intelligence Reform and Terrorism Prevention Act were the most sweeping national security reforms since the early years of the Cold War. While it remains unclear whether these reforms adequately address the weaknesses 9/11 exposed, the time for modifying bureaucratic wiring diagrams is over—the current system must be made to work. Policymakers, and especially those tasked with oversight on Capitol Hill, need to ensure that the spirit and intent of the intelligence and homeland security reforms are being followed. Top-heavy bureaucracies need to become flatter, more networked organizations.

Meanwhile, the Department of Defense must also transform itself for a long war. The men and women of the U.S. military continue to perform heroically overseas, adapting even while engaged in hostilities. The recent Quadrennial Defense Review is notable for describing the challenges of irregular warfare and the types of capabilities required to meet the threat, as well as for making specific programmatic recommendations. Especially encouraging is the intensified focus on increasing the size of special operations forces and the enhanced language and cultural training provided to all soldiers.

However, five years into major combat operations in Afghanistan and Iraq, our nation's armed forces are under enormous strain. Army leaders now consider all nondeployed U.S. Army Brigade Combat Teams in the United States, both active and National Guard, to be unready for operations. Persistent equipment and personnel shortfalls, as well as recent funding cuts, risk leaving the nation without the military capabilities it needs to respond to natural disasters, terrorist attacks, or an unexpected military crisis in the Middle East, on the Korean peninsula, or elsewhere. National leaders need to honestly debate whether the country can continue to prosecute multiple overseas operations without increasing the size of U.S. ground forces. At the very least, funding, personnel, and equipment shortfalls need to be addressed urgently to reduce the current level of strategic risk to the nation.

By far the most glaring gap between U.S. strategy and capabilities is the underdevelopment of noncoercive instruments of statecraft. During the Cold War, the United States constructed a wide range of nontraditional tools to fight the ideological struggle against the Soviet Union. From the U.S. Information Agency to Radio Free Europe, the Voice of America, and the U.S. Agency for International Development, Americans saw fit to invest heavily in public diplomacy, political warfare, and economic development capabilities. Moreover, large aid programs like the Marshall Plan, and international financial institutions like the General Agreement on Tariffs and Trade and the International Monetary Fund, helped to shore up Europe and strengthen its political institutions against communism. Five years into this current conflict however, the United States has failed to invest resources commensurate with the challenge posed by an enemy operating primarily on the battlefield of ideas.

There have been several recent attempts to address some of these shortfalls. Secretary of State Condoleezza Rice's Transformational Diplomacy initiative is promising, as it focuses on shifting the State Department's bureaucratic center of gravity from its Washington, D.C., headquarters to the diplomatic front lines. Additionally, the initiative creates career incentives that encourage regional specialization, work in front-line postings in countries emerging from conflict and instability, and expertise in public diplomacy. The administrator of the U.S. Agency for International Development is leading a high-level review of U.S. foreign assistance tools, which should be a valuable contribution to rationalizing both foreign aid and security assistance programs under a clear strategic framework.

But if the wars in Afghanistan and Iraq have taught us anything, it is that the military cannot be expected to bear the entire burden of state reconstruction. From agriculture to education to legal, health care, and governance systems, U.S. civilian agencies need more robust, effective, deployable capabilities to build capacity in weak or failing states. While the State Department took a good first step by creating the Office of Reconstruction and Stabilization, the administration and Congress need to expand and resource this office appropriately in order to create a deployable civilian cadre that is able to project and sustain needed civilian capabilities to the long war's front lines. If such a capability cannot find a home in the State Department, a new field agency should be formed to provide the operational culture, career opportunities, and support for this critical cadre.

The National Security Council (NSC) has an indispensable role to play in the long war by ensuring that agency disputes are aired and resolved at appropriate levels and in a timely manner. In the complex and dynamic twenty-first century security environment, the NSC needs to go beyond its traditional role of preparing decisions for the president and be responsible for ensuring that presidential intent is realized through the actions of all the agencies. This means more active orchestration of planning as well as more vigilant oversight of operations.

Finally, in an era when the United States will inevitably require agencies to work together seamlessly in complex, rapidly changing and often hostile environments, the government lacks a cadre of professionals who are conversant in the multiple bureaucratic languages and cultures that make interagency operations so difficult. There is, for example, a tendency by civilian officials to view military planning and orders as overly complex and a tendency by military officers to view their civilian counterparts as lacking any real understanding of what operations in a hostile environment require. The United States needs to develop a dedicated professional cadre of national security leaders.

In 1986, the Goldwater-Nichols legislation ushered in a new era in the Department of Defense, primarily by requiring military officers to gain experience in joint environments in order to advance to the most senior ranks. The joint service incentive was a catalyst for a dramatic cultural change in the Department of Defense that has resulted in a more effective and powerful military. The United States' civilian agencies need a similar system that ties advancement to interagency experience to enable a vital cultural and professional shift.

Five years after 9/11, the challenge posed by Islamist terrorism has not ended. Though the United States has yet to be attacked again, there is no analytical basis from which to conclude that the threat has diminished. As leaders and policymakers take stock of all that has occurred over the last five years, it is helpful to consider the character of the last strategy against a dangerous ideology. While the Cold War against the Soviet Union posed a very different challenge to the United States, the nature of our response holds the key to victory in this war as well. For all the debate and controversy over foreign policy throughout the Cold War, this country successfully employed a strategy against its foe that was global in scope and integrated across departments and agencies. The United States is five years into another long war against a dangerous ideology, and our strategy is not global enough and not integrated enough. We can, and must, do better.

ABOUT THE CONTRIBUTORS

Daniel Benjamin is a senior fellow in the CSIS International Security Program. He previously served on the National Security Council staff as a special assistant to the president and as director for transnational threats.

Shawn Brimley is a research associate in the CSIS International Security Program. Prior to joining CSIS, he was pursuing graduate studies in security policy at the Elliott School of International Relations at George Washington University.

Mary DeRosa is a senior fellow in the CSIS Technology and Public Policy Program. Previously, she served on the National Security Council staff as special assistant to the president and legal adviser.

Michèle Flournoy is a senior adviser in the CSIS International Security Program. Previously, she was a principal deputy secretary of defense for strategy and threat reduction and deputy assistant secretary of defense for strategy.

David Heyman is director and senior fellow in the CSIS Homeland Security Program. Previously, he served as a senior adviser to the U.S. secretary of energy and at the White House Office of Science and Technology Policy, working on a wide range of national security and international affairs.

Aidan Kirby is a research associate in the CSIS International Security Program. Previously, she was a graduate student at the Patterson School of International Affairs at Carleton University in Ottawa.

James Lewis is director and senior fellow in the CSIS Technology and Public Policy Program. Before joining CSIS, he was a career diplomat and worked on a wide range of national security and intelligence issues.

Mary Beth Nikitin is a fellow in the CSIS International Security Program. Earlier, she worked at the UN Department for Disarmament Affairs in New York and at the Center for Nonproliferation Studies in Monterey, California.

Eric Ridge is program coordinator for the CSIS Homeland Security Program. Before joining CSIS, he was editor-in-chief of the *Johns Hopkins News-Letter* and spent time at the Brookings Institution and the American Foreign Service Association.

Thomas Sanderson is deputy director and fellow in the CSIS Transnational Threats Project. Prior to joining CSIS, he served as a defense analyst with SAIC, where he conducted studies of terrorist groups for the U.S. Defense Intelligence Agency.

Julianne Smith is deputy director and senior fellow in the CSIS International Security Program. Before joining CSIS, she served as program officer for the Foreign Policy Program at the German Marshall Fund of the United States.

Karin von Hippel is codirector and senior fellow in the CSIS Post-Conflict Reconstruction Project. Previously she was a senior research fellow at the Centre for Defence Studies, King's College London, and spent several years working for the United Nations and the European Union in Somalia and Kosovo.